The Best BIRTHDAY

by Lynne Coulter
illustrated by Debbie Mourtzios

Harcourt
SCHOOL PUBLISHERS

Printed in Mexico

ISBN 10: 0-15-350649-0
ISBN 13: 978-0-15-350649-9

Ordering Options
ISBN 10: 0-15-350599-0 (Grade 2 On-Level Collection)
ISBN 13: 978-0-15-350599-7 (Grade 2 On-Level Collection)
ISBN 10: 0-15-357830-0 (package of 5)
ISBN 13: 978-0-15-357830-4 (package of 5)

SO-ASC-402

2 3 4 5 6 7 8 9 10   050   15 14 13 12 11 10 09 08 07

Mom's birthday was only four days away.

"How can we celebrate Mom's birthday?" asked Todd.

"We could take her ice skating," said Tay.

"I know! Let's take her to see the circus," said Jasmine.

"Let's take her to the theater to see a play," said Dad. "Mom loves plays."

4

Todd looked at the newspaper. "There are lots of plays," he said.

Todd read a review about a play called *The Giant Bug*.

"A giant bug takes over a city, and the people have to escape."

"That play will be too frightening," said Jasmine. "Mom won't like it."

"Well, what about this play instead?" said Todd. "It's called *Lost in the Jungle*. It's set in a jungle far away. Some young elephants are lost and can't find their way home."

"That play will be too sad,"
said Tay. "Mom won't like that play
at all."

"I think Mom would like to see
a funny play," said Dad.

"There are no funny plays,"
said Todd.

"I've got a great idea!" said Jasmine. "Gather around, and I'll tell you."

Everyone thought that her idea was perfect, except for Todd.

"I don't know," said Todd. "I hope it's the sort of birthday present Mom will like."

The family planned to do a play
of their own to surprise Mom.

On the first day, they wrote
the script.

On the next day, they painted
and pasted.

On the day before Mom's birthday, they all dressed up in funny costumes and practiced the play.

"I hope Mom will like the play," said Todd.

On Mom's birthday, the surprise was ready.

"Happy birthday!" shouted everyone as Mom came in the room.

"We would like to present an enchanting play called *The Very Funny Family Day Out*," said Dad.

"We wrote this play ourselves," said Todd. "I hope you like it!"

"The family will all sit on one big, long bike, like this," said Jasmine.

"They will travel to lots of funny places," said Tay. "Sometimes, the kids will even forget to pedal!"

"This is just the sort of play that I will like!" said Mom. "I'm thrilled with my birthday surprise."

They made sure Mom was cozy in her favorite chair beside the fire.

The play began. It was very funny, and Mom laughed and laughed.

"This is the best birthday present I've ever had," she said.

"I knew you would like it," said Jasmine.

"We can write another play next year!" said Todd.

14

Think Critically

1. If you were Mom, how would you have felt when you saw the play?

2. Why did Dad and the children perform their own play?

3. In order, describe the things the family did to prepare for the play.

4. What was the setting for the story?

5. Would you like to be in a play? Why or why not?

 Language Arts

Write a Paragraph Read page 12 again. Write a paragraph about where the family went on their travels.

School-Home Connection Talk about *The Best Birthday* with a family member. Then talk about the different kinds of plays or movies that you have seen.

Word Count: 410